Lessons From a Father to His Son: Unlocking Proverbs
Paul A. Blake

COPYRIGHT

Dedication

I dedicate this book to all the young men who are striving to discover their life's purpose. In a world where so much negative surrounds us, positive words spark new growth. Young men, you are God's heritage, and He wants to unleash your greatness. I pray these words will help you walk in the ways of God and become a man after His own heart.

You are powerful, and there is no limit to your potential. These words are to remind you that there is nothing you cannot accomplish if you put your mind to it. As a young man, the decisions you make now can begin the change of future generations. These words have helped to shape my life, and I hope they will be useful in your quest for a life of purpose.

Introduction

My son, I want to pass on some lessons I have learned in life, hoping they will help you shape the man that you are becoming. I am not an authority on spiritual matters; neither will I claim to have a handle on all the secrets of parenting. However, I believe I've gained enough experience to pass on some vital information that will help you not to make some mistakes that I have. With these words, I pray you will make better choices in living your life and understand the responsibility you have to humanity. You have only one opportunity to live this life right, and the sooner you know that every action brings consequences, the better off you will be.

We live in an uncertain world, and life will not always treat you fairly. No one is obligated to you, therefore learn what you can at the earliest opportunity. Today we have a lot more at our disposal to pass on to our children than our fore-fathers did; therefore, it means we should not repeat the mistakes of the past. My son, you have the chance to sit at the feet of fathers, elders and men of wisdom that can help you pave the way to a better future, so don't waste what God has given to you. The best way I know to teach you the principles and life lessons I have secured over the years is to point you to the place that has helped to shape me into the man that I am and the man I want you to be. The word of God stands as the only accurate roadmap to life. The bible, the Book of Books, is a gateway to godly living, and anyone that takes its teachings seriously will navigate through life in the most challenging times.

My son, lessons from Proverbs is my gift to you. I draw on several meaningful verses hoping that I can adequately dissect them to provide you with instructions for life. I choose to write these words for your benefit, but if you do not commit to putting them into practice, you will gain nothing. You have many challenges ahead; you have battles that you must fight. Some of these battles, you will win, others you will lose. But win or lose, your approach to wisdom and instruction will make a difference in your quality of life. The Proverbs will help you to see life through the eyes of a God who knows the intricacies of His creation. The words of the wise man Solomon has aided many young men to make conscious decisions about their lives, and I pray they will do the same for you.

I am your father, and I am far from perfect, but I promise always to do my very best to set the right examples for you to follow. The Proverbs are where I want to begin this journey, because, in these pages, we can find a fountain of truth. When I depart this world, I hope I would have contributed to raising a godly man, who will stand up for what is right at all times. If I live long enough to see you become a man, I want you to be a man after God's heart. Whichever role I need to play to help you become that man, I am committed to doing. I encourage you with the wisdom of the proverbs, God's instructions. They are a door to godliness and righteous living. My son, these are my words to help you find your path to greatness.

"Experiencing the
Power of Words."

TABLE OF CONTENTS

Chapter One

Proverbs 1: 7 Fear of the Lord is the foundation of true knowledge, but fools despise wisdom and discipline.

My son, knowledge of God, is as essential as water is to life. The world is in this present state because humanity has lost its respect for God, who created it to be in service to Him. If you live long enough, there will be people who will tell you that God is no longer relevant to your success, but my child, this is a lie from the pit of hell. The wise man Solomon had set the record straight, declaring that reverence for God is where knowledge begins. We are free to either agree or disagree, but it does not change the truth, it is in your best interest to live by these words.

A wise person will accept the fact that there must be some entity higher than them that controls the affairs of this world. Only a fool will harbour any notion that they are in total control of what goes on around them. My son, fools think that they have the upper hand in all things, but the person with wisdom understands that God is the author and finisher of our faith. My son, fear the Lord and gain wisdom so that your days on earth will be better. If you turn aside from God's discipline, you will suffer the consequences.

In this life, you will know many useful things, but if you do not know God, you will be like a tree without roots. Seek after that, which will help you extend your life and forget about the non-essentials. I write to you my son, hoping you appreciate God is everything, and without Him, we can do nothing that will be meaningful. Commit His words to your mind and watch your life transform before your eyes. Even when the world tries to tell you that God is outdated, remember the good proverb that speaks about the fear of God and its connection to wisdom.

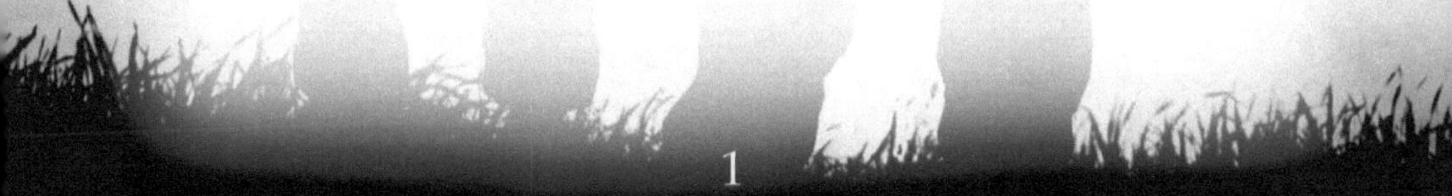

Chapter Two

Proverbs 2: 20-21 So follow the steps of the good, and stay on the paths of the righteous. For only the godly will live in the land and those with integrity will remain in it.

The idea of goodness is increasingly being frowned upon by society. People equate being good with weakness, but it is a character that is celebrated by God. My son, strive to be good even when the world treats you with disdain. Being good and living intentionally to do what is right will not receive raving reviews, but do it anyway. It may seem in your eyes that only those that choose to live in rebellion against every system find success, but this is a lie the devil wants us to believe. You ought to follow the good examples that you see in the lives of those that have gone before you. Though the world may say something different, commit to a life of nobility.

Wear your integrity like a badge of honour, even when the world wants to tell you otherwise. In today's world, finding people with integrity is like digging for buried treasure. Still, my son, integrity is the foundation of a godly character. Everything around you will be about cutting corners, getting ahead by any means necessary, or cheating your way to success. But this is not what God would have you do. I desire you live a godly life in every way possible, but my son, this cannot be done without integrity. When people try to tell you it is okay to do wrong because of what you have been taught, you must choose to be a cut above the rest.

You may be told that there is nothing to be gained from doing what is right, but there is a blessing in living for God. Seek only after those things that will help you to become a better human being because this is God's will for every young man. Honour your parents by being a good citizen and honour God by growing in righteousness. Taking this position will not make you everybody's friend, but it is pleasing to God. Most times, you are going to have to be willing to walk alone and let goodness, integrity and righteousness be what defines you. All will not love you, but some will respect you.

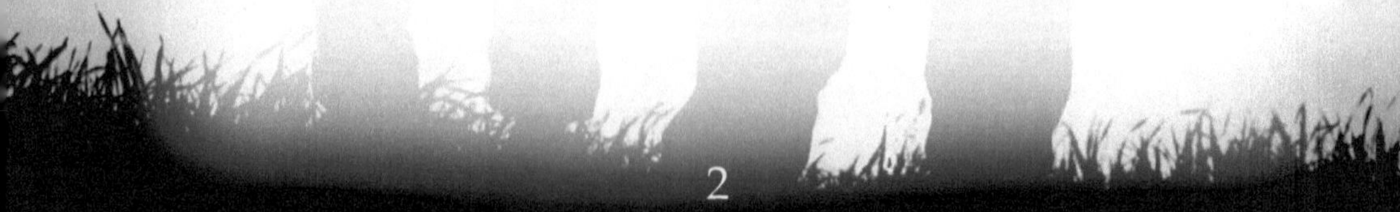

Chapter Three

Proverbs 3: 11-12 My child, don't reject the Lord's discipline and don't be upset when he corrects you.12 For the Lord corrects those he loves, just as a father corrects a child in whom he delights.

A life without chastening from the One who loves you will not do much to help you on the road to success. We exist under the authority of a God who loves us, but with that love also comes His discipline. My son, whenever we step out of line from what God desires of us, we ought to be prepared for His discipline. We live in a world where the idea of discipline is frowned upon, but without it, everything would fall apart. God does not require discipline because He hates us; He disciplines us because He loves us unconditionally and wants the best for us. When God is disciplining you, understand that He is preparing you for something great after you have learned the lesson He is teaching.

As long as you remain someone's child, there will be a need for you to be disciplined at some point. As you go through life, you will not always make the best choices or do the right things. Sometimes you will act out of selfishness, at other times out of ignorance, and sometimes you will act because of poor insight. Whatever the case may be, the need for discipline will come into play; this makes life so exciting. Whenever you find yourself in need of discipline, whether from God, your heavenly father or your biological father, don't rebel, accept it and grow from it.

The person who truly loves will not discipline you to cause harm or destruction. If a father loves you, he disciplines because he has a desire to see crooked paths become straight. A father who allows his son to go without discipline is setting him up for a lifetime of failure. A father who disciplines does not need to live in fear of the choices his son will make about his life. The thing about discipline is that if done correctly, it builds a bond of trust that is unbreakable even through difficult circumstances. So my son, because I love you as much as God loves you, I will discipline you when it is needed so that you can live a long and healthy life.

Chapter Four

Proverbs 4: 3- 4 For I too was once my father's son, tenderly loved as my mother's only child. 4 My father taught me, "Take my words to heart. Follow my commands, and you will live.

A good father has a powerful influence over the life of his son. A young man who is under the instructions of his father will be educated in the ways of righteousness. My son, though sometimes our instructions to you may come across as harsh, it is not our desire to tear you down but to prepare you for a world that takes no prisoners. We have lived this life before and don't want to see you make the mistakes we did, so listen to words of wisdom. A godly father will impact the life of his son in ways that seal his destiny, and his son will praise him for it. Even when we speak in tones that seem to be harsh, know that we always have your best interest in mind.

My son, heed the wisdom of your father and your life will reap the benefits. Your father does not have to be a man of superior intellect to breathe words of wisdom over your life. He only needs to be a man that understands he is not perfect and is dependent on the Creator to guide you in how to live. He will not always speak the words you want to hear, but he will commit to saying what you need to hear, so your life can be pleasing to God. Your father's commandments are not meant to take you away from enjoying life, but to save you from having to live with the misery of bad decisions.

Even though we cannot guarantee how long any of us will live, heeding the words of your father is a promise from God for an extension. When you follow the instructions of your father, the possibility of you being able to make more conscious decisions is significantly increased. A father's pride can be seen in a son who pays attention to his instructions and acts accordingly. My son, you may be told by others that you don't have to do this because times have changed, but the words of God can never be outdated. I am teaching you things that you will need to navigate this life, so pay close attention and learn from me.

Chapter Five

Proverbs 5: 15 Drink water from your own well — share your love only with your wife.

As you grow into a young man, your eyes will drift to the beauty of women around you. There probably is no more magnificent creation from God than the radiance of the fairer sex. Women are genuinely marvellous, and like flowers in a garden, there is a variety from which to pick. My son, find that one flower that captures your attention and give all your effort to nurture it into something glorious. Though there are many women, only one will be able to steal your breath away every time you see her in bloom. Don't fall into the trap of thinking that you can live like a bee going from flower to flower. Find a virtuous woman and learn how to treat her right.

The world is full of beautiful women, my child, but there is only one woman who will be able to hold your attention and keep you grounded. The way of the world is for young men to indulge in sleeping with as many women as they can conquer, but this is neither healthy nor wise. As you grow, women will throw themselves at your feet, don't allow yourself to be fooled by this; it is a trap from the devil. When you find that woman who will give you her all, learn how to love her like there is no tomorrow. Women will come and go as you journey through life, but only one will be able to make your heart skip a beat every time you see her.

My son, keep your eyes fixed on your wife; many men have lost their souls paying attention to the treasures of other men. The wise man Solomon knew that it was folly to give your energy to who does not belong to you, don't allow this lesson to be wasted on you, my son. Love your own woman, cherish her like the rare flower that she is, treat her like a queen without reservations. Don't become a victim of the foolish games that young men play. It is not okay to fly from flower to flower. Many young men have fallen prey to the devil's devices. They are destroyed because they never understood the value of giving themselves to only one woman.

It would indeed be a tragedy if such a valuable lesson were lost on you because you chose not to heed words of wisdom. Many before you have tried to pursue the love of more than one women and have lost their way. The wise King Solomon sums it up and declares that such a pursuit only allows the human heart to come to one conclusion, that all is vanity. God will send that woman to you who will be your distraction for life. When you find her, give her everything you've got, hold nothing back and it will be well with you. My son, don't spend all your strength thinking you have the power to please all women.

Chapter Six

Proverbs 6: 6-7 Take a lesson from the ants, you lazybones. Learn from their ways and become wise.

Someone said procrastination is the thief of time and it is the truth. Time will not always be available; you can choose to live your life, believing that you have all the time in the world to do the things you want. You can choose not to pay attention to the essential things in life. You can even decide not to make preparations for your future because it is up to you to do whatever you choose to do. But there is something that you must always remember, the things you put off today may come back to haunt you tomorrow. Don't fool yourself into believing that time will always be on your side. Prepare for tomorrow by doing the best you can do today.

Time wasted cannot be regained, so value the time that you have and do all you can while you have the strength to do it. My son, there will come a time in our life when things around you will change. You will discover that the things which once came so naturally to you, gradually become challenging. You will find your strength failing, and even your brain may not be as sharp as it used to be. You cannot afford the luxury of living a wasted life, because you don't know what the future has in store for you. The ant doesn't know how harsh the winter will be, so he makes preparations. Do likewise, because life has a way of changing and often catches us off-guard.

You may not control the storm that is coming, but you can make the preparations so that you are not hit too hard. Notice ants build their nests below ground; therefore, the possibility of them being flooded out is real. However, this does not stop them from always living in preparation mode. There will be a time to enjoy the fruits of your labour, but while you are looking forward to that, be wise and prepare for the hard times that will come your way. The time will come when you will want to look back on what you accomplished while you had the time. If you have not been making preparations, then there will be nothing worth looking back on.

Chapter Seven

Proverbs 7: 1 Follow my advice, my son; always treasure my commands. 2 Obey my commands and live! Guard my instructions as you guard your own eyes.

Growing up as a child in the country, I recall that some of the most valuable advice I got came from the surrounding elders. Their wisdom was almost always on point, and I appreciate the lessons they have passed on to me. There is a reason older people are wise; it is because of their years of experience in navigating the various areas of life. The knowledge they can pass on to the generations that come after them is priceless. They may not always be right in everything that they say or do, but one thing is sure, they know more about living than those who have just understood what it means to live.

My son, trust in the wisdom of your elders; you will not regret doing it. You are living a life others have lived before you, and you can learn something from them. You don't have to repeat their mistakes or failings because through them you will have enough information to make better decisions. Some will try to make you believe that your elders have outlived their usefulness, but this my son is another ploy of the devil. The elders among us still have much to contribute to our journey before they depart from this earth. Never discount the value of the wisdom and instruction you can receive from your elders to help you along the way.

Follow the advice of your elders, and you will survive many tough days ahead. Keep their instructions close to your heart and remember them in times of difficulty. Put them into practice and watch your life unfold before your eyes into a life that honours God. Cherish the wisdom of the old as if it was precious gems and your life will witness the reward. My son, advice from elders whether they are men or women will make your crooked paths straight; it will light your way in the darkest of times and give you the hope you need for tomorrow. Trust in those who will always be on the lookout for your soul; though you may not always agree with everything they say, your elders possess fountains of wisdom that will never run dry.

Chapter Eight

Proverbs 8: 8-9 My advice is wholesome. There is nothing devious or crooked in it. 9 My words are plain to anyone with understanding, clear to those with knowledge.

My son, every word of advice I give you comes from my heart. I tell you these things so that you may have the chance of living your life making better decisions than I did when I was your age. I will not try to butter you up with words that stroke your ego, but lack substance. I want you to learn from me. I may not always do the best job expressing what is on my mind, but I want you to know everything I say is with good intentions. It is not a simple task being your dad, because, sometimes; I feel inadequate. But with the help of God, I am confident that He will place the words on my lips that I need to say to you, my son.

I am not as wise as King Solomon was, neither am I striving for such a goal, but I desire to be smart enough to pass on some vital lessons to you. I will try to speak to you with clarity, void of pretense or arrogance because your life is precious. A father who loves his son will not be deceitful towards him, but will strive to be sincere in words and actions. My son, I am not an authority on matters of wisdom; I am just a father who wants the very best for his child. The words I say to you might not always be what you want to hear, but you will need to understand because they will help you in the future, so give careful attention to them.

I don't want to burden you with meaningless phrases and stories that will not help you on your journey. I want to give you words that will help you to remember your purpose for being alive when temptations become your friend. You will not always be in a position to recall all I have said to you, but I pray you will imprint them in your mind for use at the appropriate time. My son, I am doing for you what every father should do for his children, that is, to teach them life lessons so that they can make better decisions on how to live in this world.

Chapter Nine

Proverbs 9: 9 Instruct the wise, and they will be even wiser. Teach the righteous, and they will learn even more.

As you grow my son, you will become wise if you follow the counsel of those who seeks to impart wisdom to you. You will be able to make decisions about your life better than many of your peers. You will know the difference between good and evil and flee the latter if your heart is set on pleasing God. But with all the wisdom that you will gain, never forget you will not know everything, and so you will need further help in life. A wise man understands that he is always in need of learning something new, and so he will also require a wise counsellor. As long as you live on this earth, open your mind to receive wise counsel from your elders and peers. You will navigate this difficult life with fewer challenges and regrets.

You are part of a generation that sometimes I think they know it all, which is not different from my generation before you. Some of us had to learn the hard way that what we think we know is not what we know. We have had to start over several times because we did not take the time to learn the things we should have. We have experienced many heartaches and failures because we did not take the time to examine the lives of those who came before us. Some of us won't even live long enough to make the corrections to the mess we made of our lives. The things that we could have accomplished we did not, or we took the road of pain and struggle that could have been avoided had we heeded wise counsell. My son, don't make the mistakes that my generation made. Listen to the people who want the best outcome for your life.

If you follow wise counsel and make good choices in your life, you will become an example for your peers to follow. Don't fool yourself into thinking that you have all the answers for the questions of life. You will need help and guidance from several people as you move through different phases of your life. Be careful who you take advice from because not everyone will have your best interest at heart. One of the things about wisdom is that it makes you more aware of who can be trusted to give your sound advice. My son acquiring wisdom is a continuous process as long as you are alive; you will need to learn new things. You will need to be guided by the people who can teach you about life.

Chapter Ten

Proverbs 10: 1-2 A wise son brings joy to his father, but a foolish son brings grief to his mother.

My son, the greatest fear any parent has is for their children turning out to be unproductive citizens. It breaks the hearts of parents when they have invested so much in their children, only to have them become burdens to society or worst criminals. Almost every parent in this world desires the best for their children at all times. Some of us are better parents because of our unique experiences, but mostly, we all want to have the best result. You may not always agree with the methods your parents employ, but understand they have your best interest at heart. We are far from perfect, but we will try making sure you turn outright. My son, you are the joy of my life, and it is my prayer that the examples that you see in me will help you become a man that walks in wisdom.

A wise son clings to the instructions of his father and becomes the centre jewel in his mother's crown. Sometimes their instructions and guidance may not seem to make much sense in achieving your goals. But remember, they have already lived the life that you are working towards. You may have information at your fingertips because of the age in which we live. However, wisdom still outweighs the power of modern technology. Listen to your parents because they mean you no harm, even when they don't understand what it is you are seeking after, they will still be in your corner rooting for you.

My son seek wisdom and guidance from your father and mother. Every parent loves to boast about the achievements of their children because it's a beautiful feeling. No parent wants to deal with the heartache of children who have followed negative instructions and ended up on the wrong side of life. As parents, we want to stand alongside our children with pride, knowing that that small part of us has been passed on to them so they can become good citizens of the world. All this my son begins with wisdom and instruction which your parents can provide if you let them.

Chapter Eleven

Proverbs 11: 14 Without wise leadership, a nation falls; there is safety in having many advisers.

My son, as long as you are alive, you will need to have good counsel. It is, therefore, necessary that as you go about your business, you gain for yourself an army of wise advisers. Nobody has ever tasted success without being in the company of some wise people. Without wise counsel, my son, you will waste valuable time and resources in areas of little meaning to life. You must understand very early in your life that you don't know everything and will need someone to hold your hand and steer you in the right direction. We all need the wisdom of counsellors, even when we are old and grey.

There will not be a time in your life when you get too much advice, as long as it is good advice. Trust in the counsel of wise men and women; these are the persons who you can always depend on to have your best interest in mind. There will be people who will try to give you advice that on the surface seems to come from a good place. But my son, as you grow, you will learn how to evaluate whether their counsel is useful or if their motives are pure. As much advice as is given to you, remember you too are knowledgeable in some things. Therefore, learn how to trust what your heart is telling you. Even brilliant advice must be evaluated against what God would have you do with it. The advice of many does not outweigh the counsel of God, the beginning and end of all wisdom.

My son, besides wise counsel and sound advice, you will also find yourself in need of good leadership. You will need someone to give you instruction from time to time; this is a fact of life. Good advice, wise counsel, and strong leadership are a formula for success in the life of a young man. The people in your life that will keep you focused on these things, my son, please treat them with respect and show them gratitude. Few young people will be blessed to have these quality people in their lives, so if you find them, wish them long life and happiness. You will not understand the value of competent advisers, wise counsellors and influential leaders until they are not around to take you through those times when you are unsure about life.

Chapter Twelve

Proverbs 12: 16 A fool is quick-tempered, but a wise person stays calm when insulted.

Self-control is a trait that too few people possess in a world where respect for people is uncommon. My son, a wise man, is one who keeps his cool under pressure from those who would seek to destroy him. People will try to bring out the worst in you by testing the substance you are made of, but never give them the satisfaction by losing control of yourself. I am not suggesting that you will never lose your temper, but it must never be the thing that guides your actions. If you ever lose control of yourself, be wise enough to know that this can never be the way you want to be remembered by the people whose lives you affect.

Fools are quick to lose their tempers because fools don't stop to think about the consequences of their actions. My son, before you lose control of yourself, stop and think about how your actions are going to affect the lives of the people you have around you. Many times it is after the fact that the fool stops and thinks and then realizes that their actions have consequences that cannot be altered. Before you do or say things you cannot change, take the time to examine whether the outcome will be worth it. Exercise self-control, and you will discover you will have fewer things to apologize for; think before you speak, and the world will listen to what you have to say.

A wise man learns the art of staying calm even while fools find the need to speak. If you allow people to get the best of you to the point of losing control, they also have power over you. My son, exercising self-control will mean that you have to let people get away with some things, even when you know you have the power to cause destruction. Don't play into the hands of those who would seek to bring out the worst in you; it will never be worth your time or effort. Even when it seems like you cannot resist the temptation of reacting in anger; remember you are the One who will have to live with your actions. No matter how life becomes difficult because of what people say about you, always remember that you are wiser. A wise man, my son, does not act in haste because he knows there is a price to pay if he loses control of himself.

Chapter Thirteen

Proverbs 13: 4 Lazy people want much but get little, but those who work hard will prosper.

My son, the value of hard work, cannot be over-emphasized. Though we live in a time when cutting corners and doing things under the table is the order of the day, hard work still yields a high return on investment. There is an unwritten understanding in this modern world that we must be successful by any means necessary. Even if it means trampling the people in our path; but don't buy into this lie. People will try to tell you it is alright to be dishonest because everyone else is doing it; but my son, this is not true. If you are the only person in this world who is going to commit to working hard, be that one person with pride.

Hard work still brings satisfaction to the soul that does it. Yes, there are many ways designed by the devil to get you what you want in the shortest time, giving minimal effort, but rarely are the consequences discussed. It may seem like those who do dishonest things have it more comfortable, but this is an illusion that will fade away with time. When you have given your best to a task and know that the accomplishment is with your blood, sweat and tears, it brings joy to the heart. My son, do not allow the vices of lazy and selfish individuals rob you of this joy to work hard with your hands.

My son practice working hard even when no one is looking, you don't need to have a master over you to produce quality work. The world will want you to believe that only people under duress exert effort working. But if you understand the value of what you do, you will always give your best. Learn from the people around you who will not compromise what they know to be true to have a more comfortable life. Look at how they put in the hours to make sure that they produce good results all the time. My son, this is what God would have us do; He does not want us to run away from hard work: He wants us to embrace it, and He will openly reward us without fear or favour.

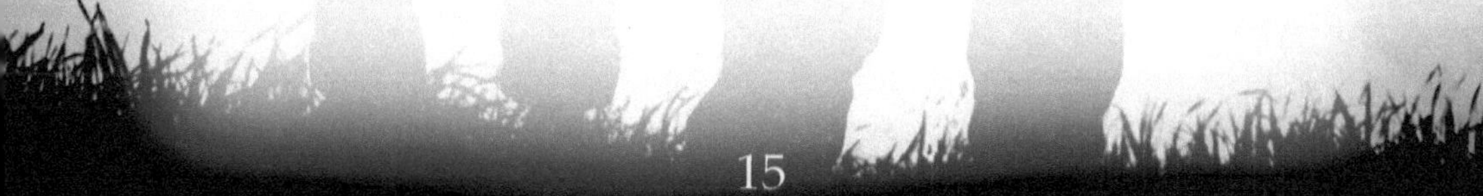

Chapter Fourteen

Proverbs 14: 34 Godliness makes a nation great, but sin is a disgrace to any people.

My son, if you desire greatness, you must also desire godliness. Sin and sinful living seem to be what makes people stand out in the world today; godliness is viewed as weakness. The average young man is pushed in the direction of pursuing things that bring pleasure and satisfaction. Godliness is usually last on the list of priorities. In the words of Solomon, a wise man, if you desire to be great in this world, you should pursue godliness. As much as godliness will make a nation great, the same is true of those who desire greatness. My son, the value of godliness in your life will not just serve for a moment; it will follow you into every area of your life.

Godliness, my son, means to live in harmony with the laws that God has for your life. To be devoted to walking in His counsel daily, even in difficulties. It is not easy living a godly life because there are many distractions to compete with, but with God's help, all things are possible. It may appear that those who strive to live godly come out on the losing end of life, but my son, this is an illusion the devil will use to keep you in his corner. The world wants you to believe that striving for godliness will make you finish last, but godly living my son will make you finish strong. Even when living right seems to provide you with no accolades, commit to living right because it is what God wants you to do.

Paul's writing to young Timothy (1Timothy 6: 6 NLT), reminds us that true godliness with contentment is itself great wealth. If you want real wealth in this life, you must first pursue after godliness. Jesus Christ calls this the abundant life (John 10: 10), the world strives for riches and fame, but those who love God strive for godliness. When we are called to recount our lives, our wealth and fame will mean nothing, but the quality of life we have lived before God will mean everything. The best life that you live is a life approved by God; my son, only this will be worth anything ultimately. Godly living not only builds nations, but it also qualifies us to be citizens of the Kingdom of God.

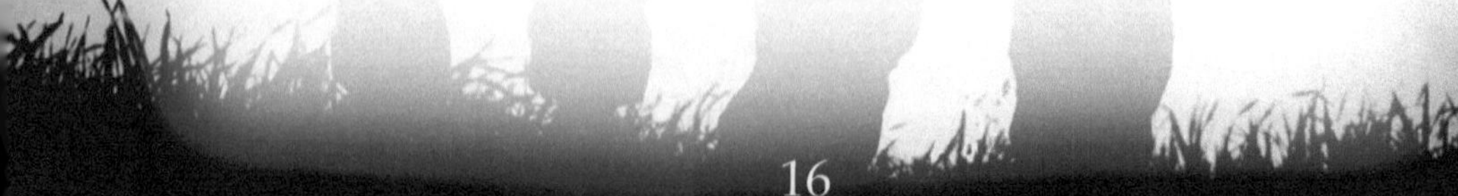

Chapter Fifteen

Proverbs 15: 1 A gentle answer deflects anger, but harsh words make tempers flare.

My son, in this world you have to pay attention to what you say; how you say it; why you say it and when you say it. James reminds us of the power of our tongues, but it is not so much the tongue that is under discussion because the tongue by itself is relatively harmless. It is the words that come from our lips via the tongue that causes problems and sow discord in every situation. My son, I implore you to weigh your words carefully before they exit your mouth and you will save yourself a world of trouble. If you are unsure of how your words will affect the people in your presence, it is better to keep what you are going to say to yourself.

Let your words be seasoned with salt, as stated by the apostle Paul. In moments of conflict, rather than giving way to destructive words because of the flow of emotions, think before you speak. If what you are going to say will not help another person become a better human being, refrain from saying it. You cannot avoid disagreements, conflict, or arguments; it's just not humanly possible or practical. People will try to pull you into ugly situations to get you to behave in unloving and ungodly ways. Usually, it is our words that deceive us.

My son, you will get the best reaction out of people in any situation by saying kind words. You will equally see the worst in people if your words are unpleasant or unkind. God has taken the time in His word (the bible) to remind us of the powerful effect our speech can have on the lives of His people. We should, therefore, pay close attention and obey Him, or we will not have the peace of God, which surpasses understanding. Strive to be like David who said: "Let the words of my mouth and the meditation of my heart be acceptable in your sight, oh Lord my strength and my redeemer". When you speak my son, speak so that you will not have to pick up the pieces, because you have been destructive with your words. A soft answer in any situation will always be the right remedy, so choose your words wisely.

Chapter Sixteen

Proverbs 16: 25 There is a way that seems right to man, but its end is the way of death.

My son, as you grow, one of the most important lessons you will have to learn is that you do not know everything. When we are young, we believe we are the source of all knowledge. We judge everything based on our opinions and most times, refuse to seek or listen to wise counsel. If you want to live a life of few regrets, it is crucial to understand that with youth comes limited experience and knowledge of how the world works. You will save yourself much heartache when you come to realise you cannot always know which direction you should turn. Even the best of us need the help of others because in deciding right from wrong, we are not always objective in our outlook.

God is the only source of all things right, whether or not we accept it does not change this truth. All of our opinions, assumptions and beliefs are subjected to God's standard of what is right. My son, we are living in an unfortunate age when matters of right and wrong are subjected to a myriad of possibilities. Everyone desires right and wrong to be seen from their perspective with little or no respect for God's hand of authority. The wise man Solomon says that the result of our faulty assumptions of right and wrong is destruction, and this is a promise from God.

My son, the only right way is God's way, nothing more and nothing less. If you want to live a successful life, find out from God what the right thing to do is; don't trust in your thoughts. Don't build your confidence upon the opinions of other people, especially your friends, because they are inexperienced, just like you. Even when you don't fully understand what God is instructing you to do, His counsel is always right, and you can trust it. Take God at His word, do what He says is correct, and you will live a long and fruitful life.

Chapter Seventeen

Proverbs 17: 28 Even fools are thought wise when they keep silent; with their mouths shut, they seem intelligent.

The value of silence is sometimes overlooked. My son, don't assume that you always need to be talking for people to hear you. We are in an era where everybody has an opinion or theory on all things that seem essential to life. It is not critical that you have something to say on every subject raised. Sometimes you must sit in silence and observe before you speak. Don't talk until it satisfied you that what you are going to say will help to educate your audience. Speak only when you know how your words will impact the lives of them that hear you. It is better to be known as a person of few words, than a fool who is continually blabbering on matters that reveal their ignorance.

There is no shame in admitting that you don't know everything. Even though people may always expect you to have, an answer for every question asked, don't get caught in their game. It is best to remain silent until you have acquired enough information to speak with confidence on essential subjects. If many people would practice keeping their mouths shut, the world would never know their level of incompetence. Be wise my son, let your speech be well informed so that when people hear you, they will see that you are someone who knows what you are about. Great men weigh their speech before they bring it to the public to be evaluated. They are aware that words, once they are spoken, are hard to recover. Be wise, my son, speak only when necessary.

You are not a fool; therefore, I don't expect you to live your life saying foolish things or being involved in silly conversations. Leave that for the people who don't know better and will themselves into believing that they are full of knowledge. It is dangerous to speak before thinking about what you want to say, so think carefully about everything before you say it. Sometimes you will have to decide that based on where you are in your life, having something to say about everything may not be a priority. Choose your moments wisely. It is better to have nothing to say than to say a lot and look like a fool.

Chapter Eighteen

Proverbs 18: 24 There are "friends" who destroy each other, but a real friend sticks closer than a brother.

My son, I must spend time to tell you about the merit of friendship. In our Jamaican tradition, it is said that good friends are better than pocket money, and there have never been more profound words. As you move through various stages of your life, you will come to understand how much good friends are worth. Your real friends are those people who will stick with you through good and bad times; they will tell you the hard truth even when it hurts, and will celebrate with you in all sincerity when you have tasted success. Therefore my son, choose your friends wisely because they will make the life you live one of purpose or one of miserable existence.

As you journey on this road, beware of those who you invite into your circle. Not everyone that presents themselves with credentials of friendship is doing so with pure motives. Some will present themselves as sheep but are wolves underneath the sheep's skin. People will come and go in your life, but a real friend will help you to weather the storms, no matter what price is required of them. My son, take time to evaluate the people you call your friends because now and then you will find yourself needing an upgrade. Don't be afraid of cutting people loose if they are not assisting you on the journey of becoming your best self. Friendship is a treasure, and like most treasures, they get better over time.

There is another lesson I want to impart to you. To have a good friend, you must also be a good friend. A friendship that is only built on one side will not survive through difficulty, and you will need it to last a long time. Friendship is not going to always be about what you are getting most times; it will also be about what you will give. Focus on what you are bringing to the table instead of worrying about what others are taking away. Be the friend that people can depend on, and it is almost certain you can rely on them too. A friend who understands what friendship means will not leave you to walk through life alone, but will hold your hand and guide you along the path that is best suited for your success. My son, this will only happen if you also remain a good friend to those who are your real friends.

Chapter Nineteen

Proverbs 19: 21 Many are the plans in a person's heart, but it is the Lord's purpose that prevails.

The best-laid plans will come to nothing if they do not have the proper foundation. We all have plans for our lives, but we rarely take the time to consult God, who is the One that controls all our lives. My son, putting God first in everything you do is what will make you successful in this challenging world. If God is not pleased with what we are doing, even if we are successful at doing it, we will not have the satisfaction that we crave. Our plans ought to be in line with God's purpose for our lives because it is Him we have committed to living to please. The elaborate plans we have for ourselves should not take the front row over our responsibility to allow Him to transform us by His grace.

My son, this world is slowly becoming godless; people are inclined to pursue only that which appeals to their nature. What God desires for us is of little concern to most people, and they are not afraid to make it known. You have been taught to seek God's counsel and trust in the answers that He provides. Follow the examples that your Christian parents and family have set for you. You have grown up observing people who have been faithful to God in every way. Not that we have lived perfect lives. But we understand what it means to put everything in God's capable hands.

God will not be mocked; don't ask Him for favours if you have no intention of being faithful. Don't plan your life and then try to fit God into your schedule; when it comes to faithfulness, God wants all or nothing. God's will must prevail in your life, or else you will fight a losing battle. There is nothing wrong with making plans for your life because God expects this from you, but you ought not to plan and leave Him out of the picture. Your success is promised; therefore, you don't need to worry, just focus on doing what pleases God and watch things fall into place.

Chapter Twenty

Proverbs 20:29 The glory of the young is their strength; the grey hair of experience is the splendour of the old.

My son, when you are young, you will take it for granted that you have all the time in the world. To be young is a blessing from God, but understand that youth fades with the passing years. Don't become so caught up with being in the prime of your life that you forget that the twilight years are just around the corner. Live your life with the awareness that every decision that you make while you are young may impact the quality of life you live in the future. The young tend to think they are invincible, but as the years are stacked behind us, life reveals that mortality can be a cruel friend. My son, while there is strength in your bones, do what is necessary to acquire wisdom. You will need it as the blackness of your hairline fades into the silver of early morning.

It is said that age brings wisdom; older men are revered for their life experiences, having gone through many storms. My son, I want to impress upon you that this wisdom that is celebrated in older men comes as a result of the lessons learnt in youthful days. If you're going to be a wise old man, you must also be prepared to pay the price for wisdom. Whatever you choose to invest your strength in, make sure the returns are worth it when your youthful days are behind you. Too many times in our youth, we convince ourselves we have all the time in the world to get it right only to discover that times are not always a dependent friend. Wisdom will teach you, my son, that what you sow in your years of youth is what you will reap when your back becomes bent with age.

While you are young, the temptation will be to pursue those things that only bring momentary satisfaction. Women and pleasure will seem like things you can't do without. You will have several people telling you that they have discovered the meaning of life. Some will try their very best to sway your thoughts in their direction because they are convinced they are invincible.

My son, one day, all this will fade away, and if you have not been storing up for your twilight years, you will face bitter disappointment. Wisdom teaches that you must value family and friends and a life of integrity over mindless pursuits and stuff that loses value. Wisdom teaches that godly living is worth more than a life of pleasure and vanity. Wisdom understands that as your years wind down you inch closer to having to give an account to your Creator. My son, choose wisdom because if you live long enough, you will have to reflect on the years that have gone by.

Chapter Twenty-One

Proverbs 21: 20 The wise have wealth and luxury, but fools spend whatever they get.

I must impress upon you the importance of having financial stability in your life. I know you will want to live a quality of life better than your parents and grandparents before you. You will want to afford the things that we couldn't for yourself and your children. I want all this for you, my son. I want you to be able to sit back and enjoy the fruits of your labour, even though I have discussed with you the value of hard work. It will be an injustice if I don't also teach you the importance of putting aside your resources for a better quality of life in the future. My son, don't get into the habit of spending money on things that depreciate in their value over time. Avoid using your resources to have a good time to the detriment of your future life. If you want to have a better quality of life than I had, you need to begin making wise financial decisions.

Learn how to invest your money; find out how your money can be making more money even while you are asleep. The age in which you are living is one of unhealthy self-indulgence, there is a drive to be happy at all cost with little planning for the future. You have the opportunity to make wealth your best friend if you can learn a few tricks of the money-making and wealth accumulation trade. Avoid get-rich-quick schemes that offer high returns on minimum effort because they don't usually tell you that the higher the return, the greater the risk involved. Trust only in those investments that you can understand with little explanation. Make sure that while you are in the prime of your life, you educate yourself on matters of accumulating financial wealth and you will save yourself from future misery.

A fool spends all that he has, but it is a greater fool that spends what he doesn't have. In this crazy world of instant gratification, you will meet the salesmen that try to sell you what you don't need; avoid them like the plague. The greatest obstacle to financial freedom is having a storeroom of useless things. Your happiness will not be in the abundance of items in your storehouse, but the value of your investments. Don't be foolish with what you earn, make sure it is used for the honour and glory of God who makes provisions for you daily. Before you think about investing in yourself and the pleasures of the world, consult Him for wisdom to make sound financial decisions. It is good to have all the money that life affords you, but it is better when it is invested so that your accounts will never run dry.

Chapter Twenty-Two

Proverbs 22: 7 Just as the rich rule the poor, so the borrower is servant to the lender.

My son, if you want to be rich and live a good life, you have to learn the art of creating wealth. We exist in a time where credit and spending are the order of the day, and people waste away in debt. Living from paycheck to paycheck is not something you should accept because God has given all His blessings to create wealth. Those who squander their resources will be cursed for many generations because they fail to learn the principles that the rich practice to procure wealth. You were not placed on earth to live in servitude to people you think are better than you. You are here to acquire your portion of the abundant life God has promised, and it can be yours if you increase your resources.

To be wealthy, you have to begin to think wealthy, as a poor man will remain poor if he is always held bondage by his thoughts. Credit cards and loans are not your best friends, stay away from get- rich- quick schemes like they were a contagious disease. Learn very early in life that you become a slave to those you owe for as long as you owe them. The magnitude of your wealth will not be measured by how much you can save, but in how much you are willing to invest. Invest only in things that can provide you with safe returns and stay away from the vices of selfish people. As you grow your wealth, you will invite more people into your life that will not have your best interest at heart.

You should not allow people to have so much power over your life that they can decide the quality of life you live. The more you borrow and spend on trivial things, the higher the possibility of someone else controlling your quality of life. The wealthiest people of this world are always seeking ways to increase their storerooms, so don't become a slave to them by working to fill their barns. Remember, my son, wealth if not wisely invested for future increase will dwindle or lose value with time. Therefore, put your resources into things that will accumulate in value as you also grow older and wiser. It may be difficult to achieve wealth that will sustain your life, but it is even worse to remain a slave of the wealthy because of poor choices.

Chapter Twenty-Three

Proverbs 23: 9 Don't waste your breath on fools, for they will despise the wisest advice.

My son, there are some conversations with individuals that will not be worth the breath you spend on them. Some people are in love with the sound of their voice, and you must avoid getting into arguments with them at all costs. Fools are wise in their own eyes and have little use for words of advice. If you try to counsel them, you will end up feeling frustration and resentment towards them. It is, therefore, best to choose the battles that you fight with fools with wisdom. Give your counsell sparingly and always be aware that even after you have done these things, it may still not benefit you. Trying to change a person who doesn't value good advice is like attempting to carry the weight of the world on your shoulders.

If you have a bone to pick with a foolish person, choose your words with care because they may not appreciate what you have to say. Use words that will bring across your message, but reserve those that will bring out their lack of understanding. When having a conversation with ignorant people, remember you have no point to prove. My son, fools can be very persuasive, so be careful not to get caught in their web of mindless speech. They will have you believe they can move mountains when in reality; they cannot climb a hill. The more they speak, you will realise how little they know, and if you get caught in their trap, you will end up looking like the fool they are.

Fools seldom spend time with their own company; they like to sit in the fellowship of the wise under the guise of learning. For a moment they appear like they are learning until they open their mouths and things fall apart. My son, words wasted on a fool are gone forever, so speak as it is necessary. No matter how good the advice you give a fool, it will not change their circumstances until they will listen. Because they cherish the sound of their voice, they seldom stop to listen to what others around them have to say. My son, if you ever meet a fool, treat them with the love of God, but understand changing them may prove to be an uphill battle. It makes no sense hating a fool because then you will not be better than they are, and my son, you are no fool.

Chapter Twenty-Four

Proverbs 24: 1 Don't envy evil people or desire their company.

My son, learn how to be independent and love the work of your own hands. Don't look at what anyone else is doing and what they possess and allow your heart to become covetous. People will do all kinds of things to achieve fame and fortune, but my son, this is not the way of the godly man. Don't live your life desiring to follow the crowd because frequently the crowd is headed down a path of destruction. Value your work and work hard to achieve the things your heart desire. Whatever is gained through dishonest means may appear attractive for a while, but will eventually fade into nothingness. Evil people know that their end will not be good and my son you should want no part of that. If you love the company of evil people, you must also be willing to pay the price of living with them.

Don't be too anxious to be around the table with popular people because sometimes the cost of doing so is more than you would be willing to bear. There is always a crowd that seems like the right crowd, but don't be fooled; it's just another tool of the devil. People will try to make you feel that something is wrong with you because you are not like them, but my son be comfortable in your skin. The friends you have in your youth are often the friends that will stick with you as you become older and wiser. Do not rush to be known in the circles of the influential because sometimes they have more issues than you do. People with bad intentions spend a lot of time seeking new victims to conquer, and if you are not careful, you will get caught in their web of destruction. So be very careful who you invite into your circle of trust.

People with evil intentions are a stumbling block to godly living, flee from their presence as you would from any sin. My son, you have to decide what is more beneficial to your life; is it to be a part of the popular crowd or to be known as a man after God's heart. The thing that God favours is not being able to run with the right crowd but to live out His will for your life. Choose my son to do those things that magnify your character in the eyes of the Lord, not to be celebrated by evil and immoral people. The company of evil and immoral people may seem the place to be for a moment, but in the end, there will be no lasting satisfaction. If you want to be approved by God, live your life to please Him and He, in turn, will supply all your needs. On that promise, He has never failed to deliver.

Chapter Twenty-Five

Proverbs 25: 14 A person who promises a gift but doesn't give it is like clouds and wind that bring no rain.

My son, let your word be your bond. Allow people to trust what you say when you say it. Do not be too quick to commit to things before you have thought them through, because people will doubt your integrity. Nobody wants to be in the company of a person whose word cannot be trusted; it leaves a bitter taste in the mouth. If you can't fulfill something, you have already committed to, make sure you let it known, and then plan to have it done in the future. There is nothing more disappointing than to be waiting for a promise to be fulfilled, only to discover that the person never intended to deliver. If you have to make a promise, let it be sealed by the words you have spoken, and understand that God is expecting you to follow through.

The world is already filled with selfish people, don't rush to be in their company. Be the person that is willing to stand out because when you say you will do something, people can trust that you will get it done. If your word cannot be your bond, then nothing you have on offer will be worth anything at all. When people are in your presence, they remember you by what you do and say; the words you speak may have a lasting impact on their lives. Because of this, my son, make sure you speak words that will allow the people around you to understand that they can rely on you to follow through with what you say you will do. If people realise they can't trust you, then it also makes it difficult for them to trust the people that are associated with you.

My son, I cannot impress upon you enough the power that words have in the lives of the people you will meet. When people can trust your words, they will move mountains for you, so promise only that which you can deliver. Somebody may be disappointed when you can't deliver. In the end, people will appreciate you for being a person of integrity. In the words of Jesus Christ, let your "yes be "yes" and your "no" be "no". There is no shame in letting people know that you can't fulfil what they demand of you. A promise made and not fulfilled will cause you much pain and grief, so the best thing you can do is only make one when you can see it through.

Chapter Twenty-Six

Proverbs 26: 11 As a dog returns to its vomit, so a fool repeats his foolishness.

My son, everyone in this world is entitled to making mistakes. Making mistakes is not the problem; it is not learning from them that will have devastating consequences. A fool will keep repeating the cycle of his folly until the day he follows a different path. You will not have success in your life if you learn nothing from your mishaps, so exercise wisdom in all things. You cannot control how many times you may fall on your way to reaching your goals, but the choice is yours to get up and keep going. Only a fool keeps doing the same thing over and over, hoping to get better results when they have already failed to do it that way. Don't be like the dog that keeps returning to the place he lost a bone hoping to find it.

Life is not perfect, and with the best-laid plans, you will still find yourself coming up short because of poor choices. As much as possible, try to avoid making decisions about your life that will cause you pain and suffering. If you can do without making foolish choices, it will be to your credit, but if not, make sure that you learn something from your experiences. People who don't learn from their mistakes are destined to live without knowing the satisfaction of seeing anything completed. When you stop repeating mistakes, you give yourself room to grow and explore life on a different level.

Everything that happens to you will present an opportunity to learn. You have the choice of learning or continue making mistakes. The dog that returns to its vomit will not be nourished by it. In the same way, repeating mistakes will not provide the opportunity to learn new lessons. Don't continue doing foolish things, hoping to get better results; it has not worked out well for anybody I know. When you learn from your mistakes, you give yourself room to grow. Leave past mistakes behind you and go on to better things. Don't waste time going back to the things that did not work for you. Avoid being a fool; don't relive mistakes of the past.

Chapter Twenty-Seven

Proverbs 27:1 Don't brag about tomorrow since you don't know what the day will bring.

In the book of James 4: 13-17, there is a reminder of the futility of trusting in tomorrow. The best plans can end in disappointment because there is little that can be done to control tomorrow. We need to understand that there is someone higher than us in charge of what occurs in the past, present and future. When we have this knowledge, we won't attempt anything without God's approval. As much as we can plan, things can fall apart at the drop of a hat. Therefore, we should not approach life with arrogance, but live understanding that everything is by God's will. Living to see tomorrow without God's approval is an uncertain option by which to conduct life.

My son, you are not in charge of your life. You live and die by the will of God. People fooling themselves, believing they have the keys to the fountain of life, is an illusion. Satan wants you to conduct your affairs, thinking you have all the time in the world, but it is not true. Everything that you plan to do and all you want to accomplish can disappear with the snap of a finger. Don't be foolish with your life, my son, because you don't know when the Lord will require your soul. While you have time, instead of making plans that may fail, seek how to please the Lord your God.

Your life, my child, is not in your hands but is in the hands of the One who gave you life. Everything that you are, you owe to Him and you ought to make your plans asking His will for you. Don't live like the people who don't know God. The people that make plans each day without acknowledging nothing rests in their hands. Don't live like people who refuse to serve the One who holds the affairs of the world in His hands. My son, I want you to be wise in your actions, make your plans, but understand that God is in control.

Chapter Twenty-Eight

Proverbs 28: 9 God detests the prayers of a person who ignores the law.

My son, if you love the laws of God, you also ought to do your best to obey the laws of the land. You cannot be a follower of God and not be a good citizen. As you live, you will witness people defying and disobeying the law, but don't follow them. If you want to stand before your God with a clear conscience, live within the confines of the law. God does not look favourably upon His children, who are persistent lawbreakers. He does not admire those who claim to love Him but live in disobedience. As we are subjects of God's law, we are also subjected to the laws of the country. You may not like them, but you can't please God and not obey them.

All the laws of the land are not fair; they don't all bring justice. Some will trample on your rights and the rights of others; it is not an excuse to live in disobedience. There will be laws you will need to speak against, others you advocate to change. But while you are doing this, be sure not to indulge in rebellion. Some laws will advance injustice; others will help exonerate the guilty, still, be obedient because God will have the final word. Where the laws of humanity fail, we can live in confidence that the laws of God will not disappoint us. If you want to be right with God, you also need to do right by obeying the laws of the land.

My son, living in obedience is not an easy task. People are not perfect; therefore, laws will not be perfect. Only the laws of God can be sufficient for daily godly living. Everything else that we attempt to do is by trial and error. For this reason, it is not likely that the laws of the land will take care of every situation. But even where the law fails my child, remember you are under a higher authority. If you concentrate on pleasing God, obeying the laws of the land, whether they are just or unjust will not be your problem. Don't work to live in disobedience to the system. Spend your time living your life to please God. Obey the laws of the land until you have the power to change them.

Chapter Twenty-Nine

Proverbs 29:1 Whoever stubbornly refuses to accept criticism will suddenly be destroyed beyond recovery

My son, your life will be full of criticism. Some of it will be constructive and provide fuel for growth. This kind of criticism though challenging to hear will help to mould you in a man after God's heart. Pay attention to the words of people who have your interest close to their heart. At times, their utterances may seem harsh, but they are meant to build you up, not tear you down. Never fool yourself into believing that you know so much you no longer need advice. There will always be people who are wiser and smarter than you are, whose words you need to hear. Constructive criticism is a rare gem in the life of a young man. When older and wiser people speak my son, you ought to listen and learn.

Then there is destructive criticism that is not useful for anything good. Learn how to recognise criticism that will not help you to reach your goals. Not everybody that speaks to you will talk with wisdom. You will find that some people are too wise in their own eyes, avoid such people if you want to succeed. When criticism is not useful, your heart will know it, follow what your heart is telling you. Even when it appears to be coming from a sincere place, evaluate each word spoken carefully before acting. Destructive criticism is often packaged disguised as wisdom.

Criticism, whether constructive or destructive, will only be as useful as you are willing to make it. If you pay attention to destructive utterances, it will rob you of joy. But if you employ criticism that is meant to make you a better person, it will save you from a lot of pain. Allow the people in your life who want the best for you to give you direction. Accept their advice without rebellion; you don't have to agree with everything they say to learn from them. The people who would provide information without proper direction keep at arm's length. My son, at the end of the day, what you choose to do with criticism will be left up to you, but I implore you to choose wisely.

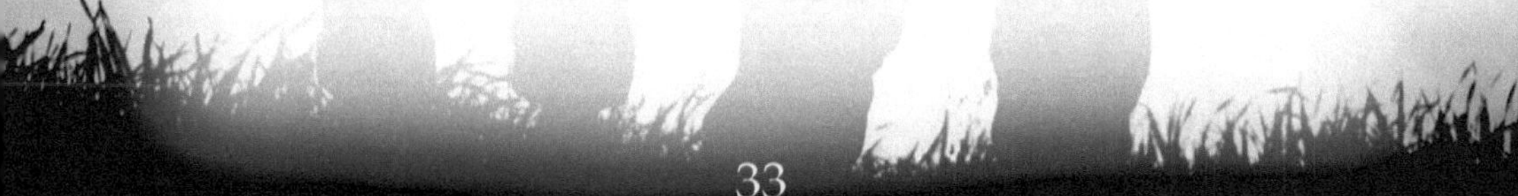

Chapter Thirty

Proverbs 30: 8-9 O God, I beg two favours from you; let me have them before I die. 8 First, help me never to tell a lie. Second, give me neither poverty nor riches! Give me just enough to satisfy my needs. For if I grow rich, I may deny you and say, "Who is the Lord?" And if I am too poor, I may steal and thus insult God's holy name.

My son, this is my prayer for your life. I want you to live a balanced life; be a man of integrity and justice. I don't want you to be poor that you may be tempted to steal, but I don't want you to be rich and become arrogant and insensitive to the needs of others either. In everything, work hard so that you can live a good life and serve humanity. Don't work to store up for yourself things that you don't need. No matter how much you own in this life, remember you can't take it with you when you die. I don't want you to be rich or poor; I want you to be wealthy in your humanity. I want you to be a good person, and that has little to do with you being rich or poor.

A rich man without God is nothing and poor a man without God is just the same. When you kneel in prayer, my son, ask God to give you wisdom. He will help you escape poverty or use your riches to provide Him with praise and glory. Work to find favour with the Lord more than you want to be approved by the world. Rich or poor, if we don't find favour with God, we are destined for condemnation. God does not desire for us to exist in poverty, and He also does not want us to be rich to the point of forgetting Him. He does not want us to live rich or poor lives; He wants us to strive for abundant living. Jesus said one of His mission in coming to earth was for us to learn how to live. Rich or poor, my son, don't forget to live.

Whether you are rich or poor will be your choice. God in His wisdom will equip you with the right tools to live an abundant life. If you don't want to be poor, learn how to work hard. If you don't want to be rich and forget God, learn the value of living a simple life. If you end poor and become a thief, you can't blame God. If you become rich and forget there is a God to be served, you can only blame yourself. My son, ask God to allow you a balanced life. If you have a lot, you rejoice, and if you have little, you still find a reason to rejoice. Be like the apostle Paul, whichever state you find yourself; your heart will be contented.

Chapter Thirty-One

Proverbs 31 Desire your own virtuous woman.

Proverbs 31 is an all-time classic; it lays the foundation for what a young man should look for in a woman of substance. My son, there are many women in the world, but only one will be suited for you. Women will come and go in your life, but there is a woman who will have your attention for a lifetime. When this woman comes your way, you must know how to recognise her for what she is worth. If not, you will miss the opportunity of having the most valuable treasure in the world. Women will try to captivate you, but there is that one woman for you who has your heart as her own. When she comes along, you ought to cherish her because she will be a rare gem in the palm of your hand. My prayer for you is that you will desire a virtuous woman to crown as your queen.

There are many women in the word my son, but all women are not good for you. Don't waste your substance chasing relationships with women who don't understand your value as a man. Not all women will spend the time to invest in a long and lasting relationship. Some women will use you for what they can get and then discard you like yesterday's garbage. Some women will pretend to love you and will pull out all the stops to keep you in their bed. But as soon as you no longer serve their purpose, they will move on to the next unsuspecting victim. When you are ready to have a woman in your life, make sure she is worthy of you.

An important question is asked. Who can find a virtuous woman? My son, she is a rare jewel, but like all good things, she is not just waiting on the sidewalk. She is the kind of woman that you will have to invest time and energy searching to find. A woman who will not give herself away quickly, but will put you to work until she knows you deserve her hand. This woman, my son, will not only capture your heart, but once she has it, she will protect it as she does her own. She will treat you with high regard, and you will never have to feel ashamed in her presence. A virtuous woman is hard to find, but when you find her, she will stay with you and give you her commitment.

Who can find a virtuous woman? My son, you can because she is waiting for you to find her. You can find her if you know where to look for her. Trust me when I tell you she will be worth the time spent looking for her. Look for her where she can be found, among those walking in the way of the Lord. My son women of virtue are characterized by a godly heart that seeks to please the Lord in everything. She clothes herself in righteousness and plays no part in evil. She practices the way of truth and does not have a place among the immoral. My son, such a woman's price is above diamonds and pearls because her value comes from God.

Paul A. Blake

Paul A. Blake is an accomplished Author, Motivational Speaker and Minister of Religion. He is on a mission to help young men overcome the stigma of negative pronouncements on their lives. He believes that young men can be empowered to discover their purpose in life through the power of prayer and positive influences. Paul was a victim of negative pronouncements earlier in his life and knows what it is like for a young man to live in hopelessness. He wants to help change the way young men think about themselves by encouraging them from the Book of Proverbs. He believes that Proverbs has a fountain of useful information to put young men on the path to success and abundant living.

Paul has been involved in mentoring young men for over 15 years. He does mentorship in schools, churches, community groups and participates in mentorship programme of the National Youth Service (NYS). He has seen the lives of hundreds of young men change direction because of the positive impact of other men, and he wants to continue the process.

LIFE LESSONS FROM A FATHER TO HIS SON: UNLOCKING PROVERBS is another impactful book from the Words to Inspire series. Paul uses the words of wisdom from King Solomon to teach life lessons to young men. He is convinced that though it is challenging being a young man in today's morally and spiritually bankrupted world, there is still hope. He draws on his knowledge, experience and a few of the lessons learned from older men to bring the book of Proverbs to life. Paul believes that young men can be positively nurtured to heights of success if they are given a chance. A holistic look at Proverbs is an ideal way to begin the journey, and he wants to help young men every step of the way.

For coaching, speaking and seminar inquiries, please contact Paul at **paulblake@wordstoinspireja.com** or visit the website: **www.wordstoinspireja.com** to about our services and offerings.

Connect with Paul:
Instagram: @wordstoinspire
Twitter: @wordsworthitjam
FaceBook@ Words to Inspire
Linkedin: @ www.linkedin.com/in/paul-blake-926a8089

Other Books by Paul A. Blake

My Story: Journey to Purpose
Words to Inspire Volume One
Words to Inspire Volume Two
40 Days to Abundant Living
Abundant Life Coaching E-book

www.ingramcontent.com/pod-product-compliance
Lightning Source LLC
Chambersburg PA
CBHW051503140726
47987CB00006B/2869

9 789769 594289